Together in Prayer
Intercessions based on biblical themes

Book 3

Susan Sayers

Kevin Mayhew

This edition published in 1999 by
KEVIN MAYHEW LTD
Buxhall
Stowmarket
Suffolk IP14 3BW

These intercessions first appeared in
Living Stones – Complete Resource Book

Unless indicated otherwise, Scripture quotations are taken from
New Revised Standard Version Bible, copyright © 1989, by the
Division of Christian Education of the National Council of the
Churches of Christ in the United States of America.

ISBN 1 84003 459 9
Catalogue No 1500317

Cover design by Jaquetta Sergeant
Edited by Peter Dainty
Typesetting by Kevin Whomes
Printed and bound in Great Britain

Foreword

A praying church is a living organism, powered by the love of God, and directed by his will. The aim of those leading intercessions in public worship is to provide a suitable climate for prayer, both for the faithful core of praying members, and also for those who drift in as visitors, sometimes willingly and sometimes rather grudgingly.

Since our God is in a far better position to know the needs of each muddle of people who arrive on any particular Sunday, it is obviously sensible to prepare for leading the intercessions by praying for those who will be there, asking our God to lead us with his agenda in mind, rather than taking immediate charge ourselves. Then we have to give him a chance to answer! You may find that a quiet walk enables you to do this, or a time wandering round the empty church, or time spent on some of the mechanical jobs at home while you still your heart and resist the temptation to badger God with good ideas.

The ideas I have provided here may well spark off other thoughts of your own. Do use them however you wish – exactly as they stand, adapted to suit specific needs, or simply as a starting point. They are a resource to help you, not a cage to imprison you.

During the service be alert to what is being said and how God is moving among you, so that you can pick up on these threads, if it seems appropriate, during the intercessions. And if you have young children present, give some thought to how they can also be praying at this time. They might be following a picture prayer trail, singing a quiet worship song, drawing some situation they are praying for, or looking through the intercession pictures provided in children's communion books, such as *Jesus is Here* (Kevin Mayhew, 1993).

I have heard it said that since God can hear the prayers, it doesn't really matter if the congregation can't.

I don't agree. In public worship it can be very distracting to be straining to hear, or isolating if you can hear only a vague mumble. Do take the trouble to practise speaking clearly and fairly slowly in the church, so that everyone can comfortably take in what you are saying. Bear in mind that nerves usually make us speed up somewhat, so speak extra slowly to allow for this.

Finally, don't recite what you have written, but pray it. Pray it both through the intentions and through the silences. Leading the intercessions carries a great responsibility, but it is also a great privilege.

SUSAN SAYERS

Contents

GOD THE FATHER

Heavenly Father

Pray then in this way: Our Father in heaven,
hallowed by your name.
Matthew 6:9

In the sure knowledge that God cherishes us,
let us pray to him now.

Heavenly Father, so full of forgiveness and mercy,
fill your Church to the brim with such holiness
that our understanding of your ways
deepens daily,
and all our work and worship glorifies your name.

Silence

Loving God:
we praise your holy name.

Heavenly Father, so wise and perceptive,
take us to the heart of all conflicts,
and give us the grace to share in the healing
between factions and nations,
guided by your Spirit.

Silence

Loving God:
we praise your holy name.

Heavenly Father, so comforting and kind,
help us to notice the needs around us,
in our families, friends and colleagues,
and respond to them in love.

Silence

Loving God:
we praise your holy name.

Heavenly Father, so mindful of our pain,
we bring to you our sisters and brothers
whose joints are stiff
and whose bodies cannot move freely;
thank you for their courage and example;
we pray that you will help their spirits to dance
and fill their hearts with joy.

Silence

Loving God:
we praise your holy name.

Heavenly Father, so welcoming to all,
we commend to your everlasting keeping
those who have recently died,
and those who mourn their going.

Silence

Loving God:
we praise your holy name.

Heavenly Father, so faithful in your promises,
we thank you for the eternal 'Yes' of Christ
which echoes on through lives and generations.

Merciful Father,
accept these prayers
for the sake of your Son,
our Saviour Jesus Christ. Amen.

Father of Mercy

You have seen the purpose of the Lord,
how the Lord is compassionate and merciful.
James 5:11

Let us pray to our loving and merciful God.

Lord, we thank you for the richness and diversity
of each unique identity.
We pray for the separate members
of this Body of Christ, and our corporate nature,
that we may be filled at every level
with the living breath of your Spirit.

Silence

Father of mercy:
let your purpose be fulfilled.

We thank you for the beauty and variety
of our landscapes and cultures, all over the world;
for starscapes and the wideness of space.
Teach us to cherish and respect
this universe we inhabit
and all those who look or sound different
from ourselves.

Silence

Father of mercy:
let your purpose be fulfilled.

We thank you for the hope
each newborn child brings;
for the gentle gifts of laughter and friendship,
thoughtfulness and sympathy.

We pray that our eyes may see all others
with your affection.

Silence

Father of mercy:
let your purpose be fulfilled.

We thank you for the patient endurance
of so many who suffer so much;
for them all we pray your wholeness
and refreshing,
your upholding and healing.

Silence

Father of mercy:
let your purpose be fulfilled.

We thank you for the promise of mercy
triumphing over judgement,
and commend to your love for ever
our own loved ones who have died.

Silence

Father of mercy:
let your purpose be fulfilled.

We thank you for all our blessings
and pray that we may take none of them
for granted,
but commit ourselves to live out
our thanks each day.

Merciful Father,
accept these prayers
for the sake of your Son,
our Saviour Jesus Christ. Amen.

Draw Us Closer

The Lord is near to all who call on him.
Psalm 145:18

Let us pray to God,
who knows us better than we know ourselves,
and understands our world.

Lord, we know we are called
to be the Body of Christ;
make us worthy of that calling,
fervent in all our prayer and worship,
loving, faithful and honest in our lives,
so that the whole Church displays
what God is like.

Silence

Draw us closer:
closer to your heart, O God.

We pray for the grace and wisdom
to care for this world we have been given as our home;
for perception in the difficult decisions,
and commitment to justice and peace.

Silence

Draw us closer:
closer to your heart, O God.

We pray for the homes of this community,
whose hopes and struggles, sorrows and fears
are already known to you.
May each household be blessed as we pray,
and may your love fill each life.

Silence

Draw us closer:
closer to your heart, O God.

We pray for all who do not yet know you,
and all whose hearts are poisoned with hate
or weighed down with despair.
May your light scatter their darkness
and bring them hope and healing.

Silence

Draw us closer:
closer to your heart, O God.

We pray for those who have died to this life
and are born into your heaven;
comfort those who miss their physical presence,
and bring us all to share in the fullness of your life.

Silence

Draw us closer:
closer to your heart, O God.

We give you thanks for all that points us
towards the beauty of your love,
and draws us closer to you.

Merciful Father,
accept these prayers
for the sake of your Son,
our Saviour Jesus Christ. Amen.

Lord of Heaven and Earth

May you be blessed by the Lord,
who made heaven and earth.
Psalm 115:15

Let us come before God our Maker,
offering our prayers to him,
through Jesus and in the power of the Holy Spirit.

We pray that the Church may be alive
to God's beckoning,
quick to obey his will
and always ready to act in his loving service
for the good of the world.

Silence

Father in heaven:
let your will be done on earth.

We pray that all leaders and heads of state
may take wise advice and act responsibly
for the well-being of all.
We pray for God's guidance
in the way we manage and care for this planet,
its resources, riches and inhabitants.

Silence

Father in heaven:
let your will be done on earth.

We pray for all marriages,
for those seeking marriage partners
and those whose marriages are under strain.
We pray for all in close relationships,
that there may be mutual love and respect.

Silence

Father in heaven:
let your will be done on earth.

We pray for all who are suffering
through illness, accident or deliberate cruelty;
for refugees and all who are abused;
that through the caring of human hands
they may experience the caring hands of God.

Silence

Father in heaven:
let your will be done on earth.

We pray for all who have died violently
or suddenly, or with no one to miss them.
May all who have died in faith
be judged with mercy
and welcomed into eternal life.

Silence

Father in heaven:
let your will be done on earth.

We pour out our thanks and praise
for the gift of life
and the gift of one another.
May we treat each other with renewed reverence.

Merciful Father,
accept these prayers
for the sake of your Son,
our Saviour Jesus Christ. Amen.

Children of One Father

I bow my knees before the Father,
from whom every family in heaven and earth takes its name.
Ephesians 3:14,15

As members of God's family,
let us pray together to our heavenly Father.

That as family members of the Church of God
we may show his likeness by doing his will;
that those visiting our churches
may find there God's beauty and truth,
open-hearted loving and a unity of purpose.

Silence

Father:
make all people one.

That as members of the human race
we may work together, share resources,
respect and learn from one another.
That leaders may inspire collective good,
and those with vision be valued and heard.

Silence

Father:
make all people one.

That we may give both support and space
to those we love and nurture;
that those of our own families
who do not yet know God
may come to understand the depth
of his love for them.

Silence

Father:
make all people one.

That all who come to Jesus in need
may find in him forgiveness, healing
and wholeness of body, mind and spirit,
strength to cope with their difficulties
and a constant inner renewing.

Silence

Father:
make all people one.

That as those coming to death
roll up the tents of their earthly existence,
they may be welcomed into the eternal home
prepared for them by their loving God.

Silence

Father:
make all people one.

That as we marvel at the generosity
of God's love, and his acceptance of us,
we may grow closer to his likeness
each day we live.

Merciful Father,
**accept these prayers
for the sake of your Son,
our Saviour Jesus Christ. Amen.**

GOD THE SON

The Word Made Flesh

And the Word became flesh and lived among us.
John 1:14

Let us pray to the God
who loved us enough to come and save us in Jesus.

We pray for the areas of the Church
which are weak in faith,
despondent or complacent;
that we may be recharged
with the power of your love,
reawakened to the good news,
and revitalised with the breath of the Spirit.

Silence

Living Word of God:
be spoken in our lives.

We pray for all areas of misunderstanding
between peoples and nations,
between needs and offers of help;
make us more ready to listen than instruct,
more ready to encourage than crush.

Silence

Living Word of God:
be spoken in our lives.

We pray for family feuds and difficulties
to be resolved and learnt from;
for the words we speak
to express love and respect,
with true charity and forgiveness.

Silence

Living Word of God:
be spoken in our lives.

We pray for all who have difficulty
hearing and speaking,
reading and writing;
for the oppressed and persecuted
whose voices are silenced,
and for all who have yet to hear
the good news of your love.

Silence

Living Word of God:
be spoken in our lives.

We pray for those who have died
and those who are dying now;
may your Word of life
encourage them on their journey
and bring them safely to your eternal kingdom.

Silence

Living Word of God:
be spoken in our lives.

We pray in thankfulness
for the joy of human communication
and the privilege of communing with the living God.

Merciful Father,
accept these prayers
for the sake of your Son,
our Saviour Jesus Christ. Amen.

The Good Shepherd

'I am the good shepherd.
The good shepherd lays down his life for his sheep.'
John 10:11

The Lord is our Shepherd;
knowing his care for us, let us pray.

For all who shepherd others as pastors,
and for all in their care;
for Christians threatened and under attack;
and all whose ministry feels demanding.
For a greater affection and care,
one for another, in the Church.

Silence

The Lord is our Good Shepherd:
there is nothing we shall lack.

We pray for all in positions of leadership
and influence in our world,
that they may use that power for good;
for an increase in our concern
for one another's well-being, across all barriers,
and for all who are working to build community.

Silence

The Lord is our Good Shepherd:
there is nothing we shall lack.

We pray for those who are wandering, lost and aimless,
with no idea that any Good Shepherd exists;
for those who die unaware that they are precious
and valued by the God who loved them into being.

Silence

The Lord is our Good Shepherd:
there is nothing we shall lack.

We pray for those who have died
to this earthly life,
that the Good Shepherd,
who understands what it is to die,
may bring them safely home.

Silence

The Lord is our Good Shepherd:
there is nothing we shall lack.

We pray in thankfulness
for your shepherding of us,
and own you as our Good Shepherd
in whom we are kept safe for ever.

Lord,
accept these prayers
for the sake of your Son,
our Saviour Jesus Christ. Amen.

The Bread of Life

Jesus said to them, 'I am the bread of life.
Whoever comes to me will never be hungry.'
John 6:35

Let us pray to the God who loves us,
knows our needs, and provides for us.

As the travelling people of God,
we pray for a deepening hunger
for the things of God
and a loosening of our grip
on all the wants and expectations
which prevent us from moving forward God's way.

Silence

Feed us, Lord:
with the Bread of Life.

As brothers and sisters with the whole of creation,
we pray for respect and reverence among people
regardless of wealth or status;
for responsible sharing of resources
and consideration for the natural world
of our fragile and beautiful planet.

Silence

Feed us, Lord:
with the Bread of Life.

As we prepare and eat our food each day,
we pray for those who grow and manufacture it,
distribute and sell it, shop for it and cook it,
and for those with whom we share food.

Build us up with your spiritual feeding
which sustains us for ever.

Silence

Feed us, Lord:
with the Bread of Life.

As we ask for daily bread,
we pray for those who are physically starving,
for all who hunger emotionally
or try to survive on spiritual junk food;
for those who mistrust God's feeding.

Silence

Feed us, Lord:
with the Bread of Life.

As we remember with love
those who have journeyed through physical death,
we pray that, nourished by the Bread of Life,
they may travel on eagles' wings
into the brightness of eternal life.

Silence

Feed us, Lord:
with the Bread of Life.

As we grow increasingly aware
of our spiritual hunger,
we give thanks for the wonder of God's feeding,
throughout our days.

Merciful Lord,
accept these prayers
which we ask in your name. Amen.

My Lord and My God!

Thomas answered him, 'My Lord and my God!'
John 20:28

Knowing that the risen Christ is here among us,
let us pray in his name
for the Church and for the world.

Living Lord, we pray for your blessing
on every group of Christians worshipping today
all over the world;
and we pray for all who doubt your truth.
We pray that our hearts may be set ablaze
with love,
and that we may walk as children of light.

Silence

My Lord and my God!
My Lord and my God!

Living Lord, we pray for all the areas of your world
which are torn apart by hatred and violence,
famine, disease, or religious differences;
we pray for an end to war
and a deeper commitment to peace.

Silence

My Lord and my God!
My Lord and my God!

Living Lord, we pray for those who face family rejection
if they become Christians,
and for all families divided by beliefs
or persecuted for their faith.

We pray for the children of our church
that they may grow up strong in the faith
with good role models to guide them.

Silence

My Lord and my God!
My Lord and my God!

Living Lord, we pray for those who wake up
to the prospect of another day filled with pain;
for those who long for someone
to spend time with them, enjoying their company;
and we pray for sight that notices needs.

Silence

My Lord and my God!
My Lord and my God!

Living Lord, we pray for those who mourn,
and we pray for those they love and miss,
commending all who have died
to the everlasting arms of the God of love,
in whom there is life in all its fullness.

Silence

My Lord and my God!
My Lord and my God!

Jesus, our Redeemer, with joy in our hearts we thank you
for the new life you have opened up to us all.
Help us to keep our hearts & minds open to welcome trust & seek you.
Accept these prayers
which we ask in your name. Amen.

Where Else Can We Go?

'Lord, to whom can we go?
You have the words of eternal life.'
John 6:68

We have chosen to serve the Lord.
Let us pray to him now.

We pray for those whose faith
is being challenged or undermined
by inner doubts or outside influences, *circumstance. Hardship*
disappointment, ill
We pray for those who build up our faith
and all who strive to proclaim the Gospel
in language that people understand.

Silence

Lord, where else can we go?:
only you have the words of eternal life.

We pray for our torn and fragmented world,
wrestling to equate the deep yearning for peace
with the instinctive urge for gratification and power;
that many may have the courage to walk God's way.

Silence

Lord, where else can we go?:
only you have the words of eternal life.

We pray for our loved ones;
for those who lift our hearts *cause us worry, unrest,*
and those who turn our hair grey/distress us; *dismay*
We pray for those we instinctively warm to
and those with whom
there are frequent misunderstandings.
We thank God for our opportunities of forgiveness, *and for his*
grace enabling & encouraging us to forgive those
who hurt us.

Silence

Lord, where else can we go?:
only you have the words of eternal life.

We pray for all who are marginalised,
scorned or rejected;
for those isolated through illness or imprisonment;
for those who feel that no one understands.
Surround them all with such love *+ completely understood*
that they may know they are precious to you.

Silence

Lord, where else can we go?:
only you have the words of eternal life.

We pray for those approaching death,
that through our prayers they may know themselves *+ your deep peace*
accompanied with love on that journey.
We ~~pray for~~ *trust you with* those who have died,
that they may come to know the full joy of heaven.

Silence

Lord, where else can we go?:
only you have the words of eternal life.

We thank you, Lord,
for making yourself known to us,
both in daily living , *and in our fellowship together*
(and sacramentally in the breaking of bread.)

Merciful Saviour,
accept these prayers
which we ask in your name. Amen.

──GOD THE HOLY SPIRIT──

Waiting for the Spirit

Wait there for the promise of the Father.
Acts 1:4.

Let us pray together to our heavenly Father,
knowing his love for us.

Father, we want to live your way
and do your will,
offer you true worship,
and serve one another in love.
Empower your Church to do this, we pray;
live in us; transform us.

Silence

Lord, we wait on you:
fill us, Holy Spirit of God.

Father, we want our states and kingdoms
to display your love and truth, justice and mercy.
We want to break down walls of prejudice
and build bridges of reconciliation and trust.
Empower your world, we pray;
live in us; transform us.

Silence

Lord, we wait on you:
fill us, Holy Spirit of God.

Father, we want our children
to be safely and lovingly nurtured,
our elderly valued,
our homes to be places of welcome and warmth;
empower your people, we pray:
live in us; transform us.

Silence

Lord, we wait on you:
fill us, Holy Spirit of God.

Father, we want your healing
for those whose lives are aching and weary;
your comfort and reassurance
for all who are imprisoned by fears and hate;
empower these lives, we pray;
live in us; transform us.

Silence

Lord, we wait on you:
fill us, Holy Spirit of God.

Father, we want to commit our loved ones,
who have died, into your safe keeping for ever.
Prepare us all, Father, to live with you in heaven.

Silence

Lord, we wait on you:
fill us, Holy Spirit of God.

Father, we want to worship and praise you
with our voices and our lives;
shape us to your purpose, and use us.

Merciful Father,
accept these prayers
for the sake of your Son,
our Saviour Jesus Christ. Amen.

Filled with the Spirit

All of them were filled with the Holy Spirit.
Acts 2:4.

Let the Spirit of God in our hearts plead
for the Church and for the world.

Great God of all time and space,
fill the Church with such joy in believing
that all Christians overflow with love,
compassion, generosity and humility.
Let us walk your way and live your life.

Silence

May the Spirit of God:
fill us to overflowing.

Great God of power and justice,
fill the arenas of leadership and conflict
with sharpened consciences and with courage,
so that wise decisions are made,
needs met and wrongs righted.

Silence

May the Spirit of God:
fill us to overflowing.

Great God of gentleness and truth,
fill every home with new insight
and greater understanding.
Break down the divisive barriers
and build up our capacity to love.

Silence

May the Spirit of God:
fill us to overflowing.

Great God of attentive caring,
fill us with your practical compassion;
may all who suffer be heard,
comforted and cared for.
Heal both their situation and our hardness of heart.

Silence

May the Spirit of God:
fill us to overflowing.

Great God of unending being,
fill death with your life
and the dying with hope in you.
Prepare us all for life which lasts for ever.

Silence

May the Spirit of God:
fill us to overflowing.

Great God of all creation,
fill our mouths with praises
and our hearts with gratitude,
for all the glory that surrounds us.

Merciful Father,
accept these prayers
for the sake of your Son,
our Saviour Jesus Christ. Amen.

Spirit of the Living God

*You will receive power
when the Holy Spirit has come upon you.*
Acts 1:8

May God be glorified now,
as we commit ourselves to the work of prayer,
interceding for those in all kinds of need.

In our worship,
and our openness to the Spirit of life,
in the Church's longing and outreach,
in the pastors, the ministers, the people,
in all seekers and honest doubters,

may the Spirit of the living God:
be at work among us.

Silence

In the welfare programmes
and peace-making missions,
in the struggle to uphold justice,
in the aid given to the hungry and homeless,

may the Spirit of the living God:
be at work among us.

Silence

In the loving and costly commitment
of mothers and fathers, brothers and sisters,
daughters and sons,
in the determination to forgive and forgive,
in all the lives shared and cherished,

may the Spirit of the living God:
be at work among us.

Silence

In the work of nursing, comforting and healing,
in the daily patient struggle
with pain and weakness,
and in the practical, good-humoured caring,

may the Spirit of the living God:
be at work among us.

Silence

In the twilight years and the facing of death,
in lives well lived and now breaking into eternity,

may the Spirit of the living God:
be at work among us.

Silence

In the freedom offered through forgiveness,
in the joy of Resurrection life,
in the hope of eternity,

may the Spirit of the living God:
be at work among us.

Silence

Merciful Father,
accept these prayers
for the sake of your Son,
our Saviour Jesus Christ. Amen.

—FAITH AND OBEDIENCE —

Lord, We Believe

'I believe; help my unbelief!'
Mark 9:24

As God has called us by name
out into full, abundant life,
let us lay before him now our concerns
for the Church and for the world.

Father, chip away from your Church
all the built-up layers
of complacency or despondency,
of over-comfortable familiarity
or under-active expectation,
until we see again
with the freshness and wonder of deepened faith.

Silence

Lord, we believe:
help our unbelief.

Father, we call to mind
societies and systems of our world.
Question our assumptions
and challenge our destructive choices;
break away the unnoticed scales of prejudice
which blind us,
so that our world may become
increasingly under your reign of justice,
righteousness and love.

Silence

Lord, we believe:
help our unbelief.

Father, replace our pride with humility
until we learn from young children
the lessons of wonder and trust.
Keep the childlike as a living flame
in all of us, whatever our age,
and enable us to rediscover your glory all around us.

Silence

Lord, we believe:
help our unbelief.

Father, as the sick were brought to Jesus
by their loved ones,
so we bring to you now all those
whom we long to be healed.
May they hear your voice and sense your touch.

Silence

Lord, we believe:
help our unbelief.

Father, earth-bound we grieve
at the loss of loved ones through death;
yet we also rejoice in you calling them out
into the fullness of everlasting life.

Silence

Lord, we believe:
help our unbelief.

Father, we thank you for the amazing truth
that you always reach out to us in compassion,
and always have time for us.

Merciful Father,
**accept these prayers
for the sake of your Son,
our Saviour Jesus Christ. Amen.**

In You We Trust

Trust in him at all times, O people;
pour out your heart before him; God is a refuge for us.
Psalm 62:8

As God's people, gathered in his presence,
let us pray.

For all who preach and teach the Gospel
in word and sacrament
throughout the worldwide Church.
For those who lead prayer groups
and Bible studies,
and all who gossip their faith to others.

Silence

O Lord our God:
in you we trust.

For all who are tortured or persecuted
for what they believe;
for the voiceless and powerless,
for the powerful and coercive.

Silence

O Lord our God:
in you we trust.

For greater respect for one another
as children of God's making;
for God's presence in each conversation,
discussion and debate,
each concern and celebration.

Silence

O Lord our God:
in you we trust.

We pray for this broken world – where people suffer sickness, oppression war.

For healing and wholeness,
mending and comforting,.
we all are calming and refreshing,
wherever lives and bodies ache.

we also pray for all who rest, exploited.

Silence

O Lord our God:
in you we trust.

We pray – the to cherish those.

For everlasting peace in the arms of God
for those who have come to the end
of their life on earth
and comfort for all who grieve. *+ wrap them in your love.*

Silence

O Lord our God:
in you we trust.

We give thanks for God's constant love
which upholds our being
and cradles our living in his hand.

Merciful Father,
accept these prayers
for the sake of your Son,
our Saviour Jesus Christ. Amen.

We Offer You Ourselves

Present your bodies as a living sacrifice,
holy and acceptable to God.
Romans 12:1

Let us pray to the God who loves us
and knows the terrain we travel.

We thank God for all those who brought
the good news of Jesus to us,
and all who nourish our faith today.
We pray that the whole people of God
may work in unity and openness
for the coming of God's kingdom.

Silence

Lord God:
we offer you ourselves.

We thank God that salvation is for all people,
and pray for a just and accepting world
where none is rejected, despised
or treated with contempt.

Silence

Lord God:
we offer you ourselves.

We thank God for the privilege of parenting
and of living in communities;
we pray that our homes and churches
may be welcoming and generous-hearted.

Silence

Lord God:
we offer you ourselves.

We thank God for all who care
with such thoughtfulness and practical loving
for those who are vulnerable,
and especially for the very young.
We pray for healing and wholeness,
peace of mind, protection and hope.

Silence

Lord God:
we offer you ourselves.

We thank God for all who have reached
the end of their earthly journey in faith,
that they may be welcomed into his eternity.
May we use the time left to us here
as good stewards of God's gifts.

Silence

Lord God:
we offer you ourselves.

We thank God for including us
in the plan of salvation,
and pray that we may be made worthy
of our calling.

Merciful Father,
accept these prayers
for the sake of your Son,
our Saviour Jesus Christ. Amen

Keep Us Faithful

He exhorted them all
to remain faithful to the Lord with steadfast devotion.
Acts 11:23

Let us pray now to the living God,
who always keeps his promises,
and who knows us so well.

Loving Father, keep the Church faithful
in telling the good news, comforting the desolate,
actively loving justice
and drawing many to freedom
through the joy of your forgiveness.

Silence

Keep us faithful:
to your calling.

As the Church, we pray for the world,
that there may be integrity in leadership;
mercy and justice for rich and poor,
strong and weak;
that there may be peace among nations
and respect for all.

Silence

Keep us faithful:
to your calling.

As the family of believers, we pray
for those around us now and their needs;
and for the families we represent, and their needs.
May the love of Christ be shown in what we do
and how we speak and how we spend.

Silence

Keep us faithful:
to your calling.

In compassion we call to mind
all who are locked in physical or emotional pain,
all who are weighed down with worry,
guilt or despair.
Restore and refresh them, comfort and free them.

Silence

Keep us faithful:
to your calling.

As resurrection people, we commend to your love
those who have died to this earthly life.
May they, and we in our turn, experience for ever
the joy of your eternity.

Silence

Keep us faithful:
to your calling.

As followers of the living Christ,
we praise you for the prophecies fulfilled,
the promises honoured and the victory over evil
gloriously accomplished in him
to fill our lives with hope.

Merciful Father,
accept these prayers
for the sake of your Son,
our Saviour Jesus Christ. Amen.

Hear and Obey

Be doers of the word,
and not merely hearers who deceive themselves.
James 1:22

As God has called us,
so we have come to pray.

We pray for the Church, the Body of Christ,
with all its collected gifts and weaknesses;
give us the grace to recognise
that in your Spirit we are one,
and curb in us all tendency to division.

Silence

May we hear you, Lord:
and want to obey.

We pray for the world
in all its beauty and richness;
give us the desire
to share our planet's food and resources,
to care for its people's well-being,
and to foster peace and justice for all.

Silence

May we hear you, Lord:
and want to obey.

We pray for those we love –
those we see each day and those we miss;
help us to cherish one another
as we live the loving way of your commands.

Silence

May we hear you, Lord:
and want to obey.

We pray for all victims of selfish or violent acts,
and for those whose lives are trapped in sin.
We pray for all whose bodies and minds
have difficulty functioning.
Make us more sensitive to their needs.

Silence

May we hear you, Lord:
and want to obey.

We pray for those who have died
and for those who miss their physical presence.
Have mercy on them;
may they, and we in our turn,
rest in the peace of your enfolding.

Silence

May we hear you, Lord:
and want to obey.

We give you thanks
for the loving example of Jesus,
who was obedient even to death
and strengthens us in all goodness.

Merciful Father,
accept these prayers
for the sake of your Son,
our Saviour Jesus Christ. Amen.

—— HOPE AND WISDOM ——

Into Your Hands, O Lord

My times are in your hand.
Psalm 31:15

Our God is the source of all holiness;
with the needs of the Church and the world
close to our hearts,
let us pray to the only one
who can renew and redeem.

Father, we are all too aware of our temptation
to place our trust in rules and traditions,
and we long for you to release in the Church
such a desire to serve the living God
that nothing is allowed to get in the way of that.

Silence

Into your hands, O Lord:
we commit the future.

Father, we recognise in ourselves
the universal dangerous wants and cravings
which are cultivated because they make money.
Give us universally such a loathing of evil
that there is international co-operation
and individual responsibility in fighting it
and building one another up in love.

Silence

Into your hands, O Lord:
we commit the future.

Father, may our homes, schools and churches
reflect and engender the Godly values

of mutual care, respect and responsibility,
of integrity and forgiveness.

Silence

Into your hands, O Lord:
we commit the future.

Father, we stand alongside all who are hurting
in body, mind or spirit;
all who need courage, support or practical help.
Make us willing to become
part of your answer to our prayers for them.

Silence

Into your hands, O Lord:
we commit the future.

Father, as Lord of both time and eternity,
we commit to your keeping
those who have died to this life;
that, freed from all pain, and forgiven,
they may live in the peace and joy of heaven.

Silence

Into your hands, O Lord:
we commit the future.

Father, write your Law of love on our hearts
and send us glowing with thankfulness
through the week ahead.

Merciful Father,
accept these prayers
for the sake of your Son,
our Saviour Jesus Christ. Amen.

The Growth of the Kingdom

So the word of the Lord grew mightly and prevailed.
Acts 19:20

Let us pray to the God of heaven and earth
for the growth of the kingdom.

May the kingdom grow
in clusters of Christians all over the world;
may it grow as hearts are warmed
by encounter with the living God;
nourished by word and sacrament,
private prayer and public worship.

Silence

Lord of heaven:
let the kingdom grow!

May the kingdom grow
in states, empires and monarchies,
in the crowded streets of cities
and in the scattered rural communities;
in all decision-making and all spending.

Silence

Lord of heaven:
let the kingdom grow!

May the kingdom grow
in every human shelter and home,
every place of work and education,
in each conversation and
in our mutual care of one another.

Silence

Lord of heaven:
let the kingdom grow!

May the kingdom grow
to bring peace and healing
wherever there is pain or sadness;
to bring reassurance, comfort, courage and hope.

Silence

Lord of heaven:
let the kingdom grow!

In the knowledge that we must all face judgement,
we pray for those who have died,
thanking God for his loving mercy,
and entrusting our loved ones
to God's safe keeping.

Silence

Lord of heaven:
let the kingdom grow!

As we thank God for all his blessings to us
we offer him the rest of our lives.

Merciful Father,
accept these prayers
for the sake of your Son,
our Saviour Jesus Christ. Amen.

On Earth as in Heaven

Your will be done on earth as it is in heaven.
Matthew 6:10

Let us lay down our own agendas
and seek the face of God,
and his will for the Church and for the world.

We pray for all who are seeking God,
and for the nurturing process in this church
and community.
We pray for opportunities to share God's love
and draw others to meet him.

Silence

Your will be done:
on earth as in heaven.

We pray for all who are fighting against evil
for goodness, truth and justice,
both those who make the world news
and those whose battles are known only to God.
We pray for our country and its leaders,
that this nation may seek God.

Silence

Your will be done:
on earth as in heaven.

We pray that wealth and comfort may not divert us
from searching out the heart of God;
that we may hear God's challenging
and gladly respond to him;
that our homes and communities
may sparkle with God's glory.

Silence

Your will be done:
on earth as in heaven.

We pray for the disillusioned and depressed
and all who have lost their way in life;
we pray for those corrupted by evil,
trained in hatred and twisted by bitterness.
We pray for the transforming of these lives.

Silence

Your will be done:
on earth as in heaven.

We pray for those whose earthly life
has come to an end,
and for those who mourn their going.
May the dead rest in the peace and joy of heaven
through the mercy of God.

Silence

Your will be done:
on earth as in heaven.

With thankful hearts we recall the times
when God has rescued and forgiven us,
leading us deeper into his friendship.

Merciful Father,
accept these prayers
for the sake of your Son,
our Saviour Jesus Christ. Amen.

The Truth Will Make Us Free

You will know the truth, and the truth will make you free.
John 8:32

Let us pray to our God in faith,
knowing that he understands what is best for us.

Heavenly Father, increase our faith,
that everyone in your Church
may be more ready to trust you
and move forward with you
wherever you lead us.

Silence

You speak what is true:
and the truth will make us free.

Heavenly Father, give to all leaders
and their advisers
the courage to be honest,
the will to be just,
the greatness to be humble
and the openness to learn.

Silence

You speak what is true:
and the truth will make us free.

Heavenly Father, at the door of each home
place your welcome;
in the rooms of each home, your love;
in the eyes of each person, your truth;
and in all our companionship, your own.

Silence

You speak what is true:
and the truth will make us free.

Heavenly Father, give comfort and healing
to those who are ill,
peace to the anxious,
and reassurance to the afraid;
may we know your love for us
through both the good and the agonising times.

Silence

You speak what is true:
and the truth will make us free.

Heavenly Father, may the dying be prepared
to meet you,
and the souls of those who have died in faith
live for ever in the joy of your presence.

Silence

You speak what is true:
and the truth will make us free.

Heavenly Father, give us thankful hearts
to bless your name in sadness and in joy,
knowing that you are always there beside us.

Merciful Father,
accept these prayers
for the sake of your Son,
our Saviour Jesus Christ. Amen.

Lighten Our Darkness

The people who live in darkness will see a great light.
Matthew 4:16 (GNB)

In humility and love
let us draw near to our God
and pray to him now.

Lord God, we pray that our lives
may be upright and holy;
that our church communities may shine
with goodness and love, humility and truth;
we pray for all leaning lives to be straightened up
through your merciful forgiveness.

Silence

Holy God, scatter all darkness:
and bathe our world in your light.

Lord God, we pray that many
may be empowered to recognise evil
and fight against it;
to discern your warnings and speak them out;
to notice the sparks of love and goodness
and celebrate them.

Silence

Holy God, scatter all darkness:
and bathe our world in your light.

Lord God, we pray that our households
and neighbourhoods,
our places of work and leisure,
may be arenas of praise and thankfulness,

not only in the comfort zones
but particularly through the disturbed
and difficult times.

Silence

Holy God, scatter all darkness:
and bathe our world in your light.

Lord God, we pray for those in prison;
for those leading cruel and violent lives;
for all victims of oppression or abuse;
for all who suffer mental anguish or physical pain.

Silence

Holy God, scatter all darkness:
and bathe our world in your light.

Lord God, we pray for those who have died,
that they, and we in our turn, may be given
merciful judgement through Jesus our Saviour,
and brought into the unquenchable light of heaven.

Silence

Holy God, scatter all darkness:
and bathe our world in your light.

Lord God, we pray for more thankful hearts
to bless you, because the gifts we receive from you
are so much more than we deserve.

Merciful Father,
accept these prayers
for the sake of your Son,
our Saviour Jesus Christ. Amen.

Godly Wisdom

If any of you is lacking in wisdom, ask God,
who gives to all generously and ungrudgingly,
and it will be given you.
James 1:5

Our God made us and our universe,
and delights in us.
Prompted by the Spirit of God in us,
let us pray.

We pray for the godly wisdom
that is touched by the beauty of creation,
delights in the diversity of people,
and warms to the possibilities
of co-operative prayer and work
for the coming of the kingdom.

Silence

Wise and holy God:
we are your children.

We pray for the godly wisdom
that, in observing symptoms, discerns causes
and responds to the real needs;
that strives not to control but enable,
not to manipulate but empower.

Silence

Wise and holy God:
we are your children.

We pray for the godly wisdom
that gives others both space and support,

that encourages and guides,
that knows when to speak
and when to be silent.

Silence

Wise and holy God:
we are your children.

We pray for the godly wisdom
that recognises the poverty of the rich
and the wealth among the poor;
that questions assumptions of worth
and cherishes those whom the world discards.

Silence

Wise and holy God:
we are your children.

We pray for the godly wisdom
that sees time in the context of eternity,
and death as the gateway to heaven.

Silence

Wise and holy God:
we are your children.

We pray for the godly wisdom
that lives simply and thankfully,
rejoicing in all that God is and does.

Merciful Father,
**accept these prayers
for the sake of your Son,
our Saviour Jesus Christ. Amen.**

———————— LOVE ————————

Lord of Love

Owe no one anything, except to love one another.
Romans 13:8

Through Jesus
we are shown God's compassion and mercy;
let us pray for that love in our lives,
in the Church and in the world.

Let compassion and mercy
be the hallmarks of our church life
and all its activities;
let us be noticeable by their shining
in our behaviour and our conversations;
disrupt any rules which block them out.

Silence

Lord of love:
may your love fill our lives.

Let compassion and mercy
take root in every institution, policy and structure;
let them challenge accepted wrongs
and disturb complacency.

Silence

Lord of love:
may your love fill our lives.

Let compassion and mercy
guard every doorway and fill every room;
let them colour each encounter
and drive every decision.

Silence

Lord of love:
may your love fill our lives.

Let compassion and mercy
transform our attitudes
to all whose illness or frailty
makes them marginalised, ignored or despised.
Let there be healing of all damaged self-perception,
and restoration of jarred human dignity.

Silence

Lord of love:
may your love fill our lives.

Let compassion and mercy
accompany the dying
and welcome them into eternity.

Silence

Lord of love:
may your love fill our lives.

Let compassion and mercy
blossom in all of us,
as we live out our thankfulness
to the God of love,
for all his goodness to us.

Merciful Father,
accept these prayers
for the sake of your Son,
our Saviour Jesus Christ. Amen.

The New Commandment

I give you a new commandment,
that you love one another.
John 13:34

Knowing God's love and affection for us,
let us pray to him now.

Father, wherever there is friction and conflict
in the Church,
and communities are divided and weakened;
give us a greater longing for your healing
and a deeper commitment to forgiving love.

Silence

Help us, Lord:
to love one another.

Father, wherever tangled political situations
seem impossible to solve,
wherever conflicting interests threaten peace;
wherever the ears of the powerful
remain insulated against the cries of the oppressed;
give us ears to hear your guidance.

Silence

Help us, Lord:
to love one another.

Father, wherever families are dysfunctional
or children are in danger;
wherever the daily living conditions
are damaging to health and self-respect;
let your kingdom come.

Silence

Help us, Lord:
to love one another.

Father, wherever the ill and injured
need comfort and assistance;
wherever the elderly and housebound
sit each day for hours alone;
may we bring your love and help.

Silence

Help us, Lord:
to love one another.

Father, wherever people are travelling
that last journey of death,
may they be surrounded by your love
and welcomed into your heaven,
and may those who mourn be comforted.

Silence

Help us, Lord:
to love one another.

Father, wherever the beauty of creation
reflects your love,
may our hearts be lifted to you
in thanks and praise.

Merciful Father,
**accept these prayers
for the sake of your Son,
our Saviour Jesus Christ. Amen.**

Rooted in Love

... rooted and grounded in love.
Ephesians 3:17

Let us pray trustfully to the God
who has loved us into being
and cherished us all our life.

Loving God, guide your Church
into ways of spiritual beauty and gracious wisdom.
May your word be spoken out with passion
and heard with humility and joy.
Sustain and feed us so that we bear fruit in abundance.

Silence

Lord, root your people:
firmly in your love.

Loving God, may justice and righteousness
flourish in this neighbourhood, this country, this world.
Bless those who work to right what is wrong
and mediate where there is conflict.
Raise up leaders who are happy to serve
and protect them from power's corruption.

Silence

Lord, root your people:
firmly in your love.

Loving God, we thank you
for the nurturing we have received,
and pray for our children and young people as they grow.
Protect them from evil and strengthen them in faith;
may they continue to be yours for ever.

Silence

Lord, root your people:
firmly in your love.

Loving God, give comfort and healing to all
who are in any kind of need, sorrow or pain.
May they sense your reassuring presence
and know that you are there with them,
wherever their journey takes them.

Silence

Lord, root your people:
firmly in your love.

Loving God, we pray for those
who have died to this earthly life,
and now see you face to face.
We remember your mercy
and commit our loved ones
to the safety of your keeping.

Silence

Lord, root your people:
firmly in your love.

Loving God, we thank you for all the care
and attention that you lavish on us;
make us worthy of our calling
and continue your ongoing work in us.

Merciful Father,
**accept these prayers
for the sake of your Son,
our Saviour Jesus Christ. Amen.**

Growing in Love

And this is my prayer,
that your love may overflow more and more.
Philippians 1:9

As we gather together
in the presence of our parent God,
let us pray.

Loving Father, we pray
for all who are persecuted for their faith,
and for whom following you brings danger.
We pray for those who are new to faith
and those who no longer walk with you.
We thank you for the example of those
whose faith shines out in their lives.

Silence

We are all your children:
help us grow in love.

Loving Father, we pray
for those who are forced to leave their homes,
their families or their countries.
We pray for those who, through war and famine,
must watch their children die.
We pray for your peace and comfort.

Silence

We are all your children:
help us grow in love.

Loving Father, we pray
for all the loving care that goes on in this community

and for those who crave tenderness
and are weary of the struggle to be strong.

Silence

We are all your children:
help us grow in love.

Loving Father, we pray
for all new parents and their babies,
and all giving birth today.
We pray for all who are vulnerable,
that they may be protected from harm.

Silence

We are all your children:
help us grow in love.

Loving Father, there are those here
whose loved ones have died,
and are still remembered with great affection.
We remember them now,
rejoicing in all they gave,
and commending them to your protection for ever.

Silence

We are all your children:
help us grow in love.

Loving Father, we give you thanks
for the comfort you provide in all our troubles,
and for the richness of all our relationships.

Merciful Father,
accept these prayers
for the sake of your Son,
our Saviour Jesus Christ. Amen.

SPECIAL DAYS

First Sunday of Advent

… and they shall name him Emmanuel;
which means, 'God is with us'.
Matthew 1:23

As we gather expectantly in God's presence,
at the beginning of Advent, let us pray.

God of cleansing and liberating power,
give us the courage and perception
to see ourselves as we really are,
and repent of our sin;
may the whole Church be cleansed and renewed.

Silence

Come, O come, Emmanuel:
come and live in us.

God of wisdom and truth,
we pray for the world's leaders and all in authority,
that they may lead and govern wisely and honestly,
without corruption and for the common good.

Silence

Come, O come, Emmanuel:
come and live in us.

God of love and faithfulness,
may every family be surrounded and upheld
by your presence,
the conflicts healed and needs provided for,
and every act of kindness blessed.

Silence

Come, O come, Emmanuel:
come and live in us.

God of wholeness,
bring your reassurance and healing,
your hope and patience
to all who are suffering in any way;
bring freedom to all imprisoned by hate or guilt,
and a change of heart to all who need to forgive.

Silence

Come, O come, Emmanuel:
come and live in us.

God of unending life,
bring life in its fullness to us here,
and to those who have completed their time on earth.
May they know the freedom and joy of your heaven.

Silence

Come, O come, Emmanuel:
come and live in us.

God of warmth and brightness,
we praise you for all our many blessings,
and above all for coming to save us and set us free.

Merciful Father,
accept these prayers
for the sake of your Son,
our Saviour Jesus Christ. Amen.

Christmas Day

For a child has been born for us, a son given to us.
Isaiah 9:6

As we gather to celebrate Christmas,
let us pray to the living God.

Lord God, thank you for our Church
and its people, ministers and leaders,
and all who pray.
Bless us all and strengthen us for your service
so we can touch the world with your love.

Silence

Holy God:
be born in us today.

Lord God, we thank you for our world
and all its beauty and blessing.
Teach us your ways, your love and your truth,
and let your kingdom grow and flourish.

Silence

Holy God:
be born in us today.

Lord God, we thank you for our families,
our neighbours and our friends,
for the happiness of human loving and sharing.
We pray for your blessing on all those we love,
whether present with us today or far away.

Silence

Holy God:
be born in us today.

Lord God, we thank you for health and strength,
and pray now for your help and healing
wherever people ache with pain and sorrow,
loneliness or fear.
Bless them in their need
and surround them with love.

Silence

Holy God:
be born in us today.

Lord God, we thank you for lives well lived,
and all who have guided us to you.
We pray for those who have died
and all for whom Christmas
sharpens the loss of loved ones.

Silence

Holy God:
be born in us today.

Lord God, we thank you for Christmas joy
and all the opportunities
to show our love for one another.
May our love, rooted in yours,
continue throughout the year.

Merciful Father,
**accept these prayers
for the sake of your Son,
our Saviour Jesus Christ. Amen.**

Easter Day

*Just as Christ was raised from the dead
by the glory of the Father,
so we too might walk in newness of life.*
Romans 6:4

As we celebrate the risen Christ,
let us pray to the God of life,
in whom we live.

That the Church of God
may be bursting with new life,
filled with the love
that takes even death in its stride;
that new and mature Christians together,
all in their various ministries,
may work in God's strength
for the coming kingdom.

Silence

Christ is risen:
Lord, raise us also to new life.

That the inhabitants of our planet
may recognise God's glory all around,
co-operate in the sharing of his gifts,
and cultivate the habit of caring love.

Silence

Christ is risen:
Lord, raise us also to new life.

That God will bless our homes and families,
our places of work and leisure,

with new life and the hope of new possibilities
touching the ordinary with beauty and joy.

Silence

Christ is risen:
Lord, raise us also to new life.

That all who feel trapped or imprisoned –
physically, mentally or spiritually –
may feel the stones rolled away
and new light pouring into their lives.

Silence

Christ is risen:
Lord, raise us also to new life.

That those who have died to this earthly life
may find the fullness of God's eternity,
flooded with the light of his love.

Silence

Christ is risen:
Lord, raise us also to new life.

That we may live each moment thankfully,
assured of God's company and mercy.

Merciful Father,
accept these prayers
for the sake of your Son,
our Saviour Jesus Christ. Amen.

Ascension Day

For he must reign
until he has put all his enemies under his feet.
1 Corinthians 15:25

Rejoicing that Jesus has ascended into the heavens,
let us pray in confidence to God our Father.

We pray in thankfulness
for those who introduced us to Jesus
and who help us along our spiritual journey.
We pray for one another in this church
and for all Christians, young and old,
throughout the world.

Silence

Let your kingdom come:
the kingdom of your love.

We pray with longing
for the world to be governed
in accordance with your law of love;
that all your creation may be reverenced
and treated with respect.

Silence

Let your kingdom come:
the kingdom of your love.

We pray with concern
for all the homes, schools and places of work
in this community;
rejoicing in all that is of you,
and asking your healing forgiveness
wherever there is discord or bitterness.

Silence

Let your kingdom come:
the kingdom of your love.

We pray with hope
for the healing and restoration to wholeness
of all who are ill or troubled,
damaged or depressed.

Silence

Let your kingdom come:
the kingdom of your love.

We pray with confidence
for those who have come to the end
of their earthly lives,
that they may be given merciful judgement
and welcomed into the glory of heaven.

Silence

Let your kingdom come:
the kingdom of your love.

We pray with joy
as we celebrate Jesus entering the glory
he so richly deserves, and look expectantly
towards his second coming.

Merciful Father,
accept these prayers
for the sake of your Son,
our Saviour Jesus Christ. Amen.

Pentecost

You will receive the gift of the Holy Spirit.
Acts 2:38

In the power of the Holy Spirit,
let us pray.

For a fresh in-breathing of life and power
in each church community,
which breaks down our barriers
and sets us on fire with God's love.

Silence

Come, Holy Spirit:
Holy Spirit, come!

For the grace to see this world
and its needs and problems
through the eyes of love, hope,
justice and mercy;
for the grace to abandon prejudice
and build bridges of reconciliation.

Silence

Come, Holy Spirit:
Holy Spirit, come!

For the Spirit of loving kindness
to fill our homes, schools and places of work;
for family rifts to be healed
and long-standing conflicts resolved.

Silence

Come, Holy Spirit:
Holy Spirit, come!

For the restoration of those who are sick
to wholeness and well-being;
for courage and patience in all suffering,
and for good to be distilled
from every painful, destructive experience.

Silence

Come, Holy Spirit:
Holy Spirit, come!

For God's merciful judgement
on those who have died,
and the opportunity for us all
to prepare carefully for meeting God
face to face.

Silence

Come, Holy Spirit:
Holy Spirit, come!

For a deeper knowledge and love
of the God who knows and loves us completely.

Merciful Father,
**accept these prayers
for the sake of your Son,
our Saviour Jesus Christ. Amen.**

Trinity Sunday

In the name of the Father,
and of the Son and of the Holy Spirit.
Matthew 28:19

Let us pray to the Father
through the Son
and in the power of the Holy Spirit.

Lord God, may the Church reflect
your community and unity;
may there be Godly harmony, shared ministry,
mutual support and encouragement in the faith.

Silence

Father, Son and Holy Spirit:
bind us together in love.

Lord God, may the world's leaders
seek not personal power but the public good;
may conflicts be faced honestly
and needs recognised and met;
may all our communities be built up
on what is good, true, just and right.

Silence

Father, Son and Holy Spirit:
bind us together in love.

Lord God, may there be love and respect
for one another in every household;
may there be mutual support
and thoughtfulness, consideration and trust.

Silence

Father, Son and Holy Spirit:
bind us together in love.

Lord God, may the hearts' cries for help be heard;
the tears collected and the fears quieted;
may suffering be eased and guilt erased
through your healing love.

Silence

Father, Son and Holy Spirit:
bind us together in love.

Lord God, may the dead rise
to new and eternal life,
freed from their aching and restored for ever.

Silence

Father, Son and Holy Spirit:
bind us together in love.

Lord God, we pour out to you
our praise and wonder
at the hidden mysterious holiness
of your Being, so full of glory and love!

Merciful Father,
**answer these prayers
for the sake of your Son,
and in the power of the Holy Spirit. Amen.**

All Saints' Day

As God's chosen ones, holy and beloved,
clothe yourselves with
compassion, kindness, humility, meekness and patience.
Colossians 3:12

Let us pray to the God
who can love sinners into saints.

Thank you, Father, for the faithful prayers
of so many over the generations;
for the lifetimes of quiet godliness;
for the struggles bravely borne
and the witness of strong faith.

Silence

Lord, make us all:
worthy of our calling.

Thank you, Father, for all peace-makers
and those who strive for justice and reconciliation;
thank you for those who work to relieve suffering
and manage the world's resources more fairly.

Silence

Lord, make us all:
worthy of our calling.

Thank you for the blessing and hope
of each new generation;
for the richness of good friendships,
the happiness of those in love,
and the comfort of prayer support.

Silence

Lord, make us all:
worthy of our calling.

Thank you for the care and attention
given to those in pain and ill health;
for the example of those
whom it is always a pleasure to visit,
in spite of their suffering;
for those who allow their suffering
to be used for some good.

Silence

Lord, make us all:
worthy of our calling.

Thank you for the love and encouragement
we have received through the years
from those who have died in faith
and are remembered with great affection.

Silence

Lord, make us all:
worthy of our calling.

Thank you for all the saints of heaven
who join us as we praise God
in all his holiness.

Merciful Father,
**accept these prayers
for the sake of your Son,
our Saviour Jesus Christ. Amen.**

—————— INDEXES ——————

Topical Index

THE COMMUNITY

PEOPLE IN NEED

Forgiveness	8, 17, 20, 28, 36, 37, 46, 60, 77, 82
Guilt	47, 77, 87
Hate	13, 33, 57, 77
Healing	11, 13, 17, 33, 35, 37, 40, 45, 55, 59, 67, 71, 77, 79, 82, 83, 85, 87
Hunger	25
Illness	15, 29, 59, 67, 69, 83, 85
Learning difficulties	21, 49
Loneliness	27, 29, 69, 79
Lost	22
Marginalised	29, 67
Nursing	37
Pain	9, 27, 37, 47, 53, 55, 61, 71, 79, 85, 89
Patience	11
Peace	45, 55, 59
Persecution/oppression	21, 26, 61, 68
Physical disability	9, 21, 49
Prisoners	29, 61
Violence	15, 49, 61
Weariness	33
Worry	47

N.B. Each set of prayers includes intercessions for the dying and those who have died.

Biblical Index